Hans zimmer

HANS ZIMMER BIOGRAPHY

Music as a Storytelling Force - The Creative Mind Behind the Films You Love

Kelvin H. Christian

Hans zimmer

All rights reserved. No part of this book may be reproduced, distributed, or transmitted in any form or by any means, including photocopying, recording, or other electronic or mechanical methods, without the prior written permission of the publisher, except in the case of brief quotations embodied in critical reviews and specific other noncommercial uses permitted by copyright law.

Copyright @ 2024 by kelvin H. Christian

Hans zimmer

Disclaimer

This book contains information that is solely meant to be educational. Despite their best efforts to present accurate and current information, the author and publisher disclaim all expressed and implied representations and warranties regarding the availability, completeness, accuracy, reliability, suitability, or suitability of the content contained herein for any purpose. The publisher and the author disclaim all responsibility for any loss or harm, including without limitation, consequential or indirect loss or damage, or any loss or damage at

Hans zimmer

all resulting from lost profits or data resulting from using this book.

Hans zimmer

Table of contents

INTRODUCTION

CHAPTER 1: THE EARLY YEARS – A CHILDHOOD IN GERMANY

Discovering Music

From Keyboards to Composing

CHAPTER 2: BREAKING INTO THE INDUSTRY – MOVING TO LONDON

Early Collaborations and Influences

The Breakthrough with Rain Man

CHAPTER 3: CRAFTING A UNIQUE SOUND – SYNTHESIZERS AND THE ZIMMER STYLE

Combining Classical and Modern Sounds

Reinventing Film Music

CHAPTER 4: COLLABORATING WITH FILMMAKERS – WORKING WITH RIDLEY SCOTT: GLADIATOR

The Iconic Partnership with Christopher Nolan

Hans zimmer

Scoring The Lion King and Winning an Oscar
CHAPTER 5: MUSIC AS A STORYTELLING TOOL – HOW ZIMMER'S SCORES SHAPE FILM NARRATIVE
Creating Emotion Through Sound
Building Suspense and Drama
CHAPTER 6: THE TECHNOLOGY OF SOUND – INNOVATIONS IN MUSIC PRODUCTION
The Role of Digital Instruments
Experimenting with New Sounds
CHAPTER 7: ZIMMER'S MOST ICONIC SCORES – INCEPTION: DREAM LAYERS IN MUSIC
The Epic Journey of Interstellar
The Heroic Themes of The Dark Knight Trilogy
From Fantasy to Reality: Dune

CHAPTER 8: A GLOBAL INFLUENCE – ZIMMER'S IMPACT ON FILM MUSIC WORLDWIDE

Mentoring the Next Generation of Composers

CHAPTER 9: THE LEGACY OF HANS ZIMMER – REDEFINING THE SOUND OF MODERN CINEMA

Awards and Accolades

The Zimmer Legacy

CHAPTER 10: THE MAN BEHIND THE MUSIC – A LIFE DEDICATED TO CREATIVITY

Personal Life and Values

The Future of Hans Zimmer

CONCLUSION

INTRODUCTION

To Hans Zimmer: Music as a Storytelling Force - The Creative Mind Behind the Films You Love

When you watch a movie, there are moments when the music makes your heart race, brings tears to your eyes, or fills you with hope. Behind some of the most powerful and unforgettable moments in cinema is one man: Hans Zimmer. From the soaring battle cries of Gladiator to the mind-bending dreams of Inception, Zimmer's music doesn't just accompany the images on screen—it tells a story of its own.

Hans Zimmer is not your ordinary composer. He revolutionized the way movie music is made,

Hans zimmer

blending traditional orchestras with electronic sounds, creating new emotions, and bringing depth to the films we love. His music speaks when words cannot, making us feel things we didn't even realize we could feel during a movie.

Born in Germany, Hans Zimmer started his musical journey like many others—playing piano as a child. But what made him different was how he saw music not just as notes on a page, but as a way to tell stories. He believed that music could transform a scene and that it could be as important as dialogue or action. His passion for this idea took him from his early days in London to the heart of Hollywood, where he became one of the most sought-after composers in the world.

Hans zimmer

This book takes you on a journey through Hans Zimmer's life and career. You'll discover how he broke into the film industry, his creative process, and the stories behind some of his most famous scores. We'll explore how he collaborates with top directors like Christopher Nolan and Ridley Scott, and how his music shaped films like The Lion King, The Dark Knight, and Interstellar. His scores don't just add to the films—they help define them.

Zimmer has always believed that music is a storytelling force. Through the highs and lows of his career, his passion for storytelling has never wavered. His music guides us through complex emotions, lifts us in moments of triumph, and grounds us in moments of reflection. Whether it's the haunting simplicity of the piano in Interstellar, the adrenaline-pumping drums in

Madagascar, or the powerful African rhythms in The Lion King, Zimmer's music speaks to our emotions, telling a story that words alone cannot.

In this book, we'll dive deep into his creative mind, uncovering the techniques and inspirations behind his most beloved scores. We'll explore how Zimmer's innovations in sound have changed the world of film music forever, and how his legacy continues to inspire new generations of composers and filmmakers.

Hans Zimmer's music has touched millions of people across the globe, creating moments that are not just heard but felt. As we explore his career, you'll come to understand how music, when crafted by a genius like Zimmer, becomes more than just background noise—it becomes an essential part of the storytelling experience.

Hans zimmer

So, whether you are a longtime fan of Hans Zimmer's work or someone new to the world of film scores, this book will offer you a deeper understanding of the man who changed the way we experience movies. Let's begin the journey into the soundscapes that have brought unforgettable stories to life.

CHAPTER 1: THE EARLY YEARS – A CHILDHOOD IN GERMANY

Hans Zimmer was born on September 12, 1957, in Frankfurt, Germany, into a world where music would soon become central to his life. However, his early years were marked by personal tragedy. When he was just six years old, his father, an engineer, passed away. This loss had a profound effect on Zimmer, and in many ways, music became a form of escape and expression. It allowed him to channel his emotions into something creative, rather than letting grief consume him.

Zimmer grew up in a family that valued music, and his mother was an accomplished musician.

Hans zimmer

She played the classical piano, which exposed Hans to music at a young age. While he was given piano lessons, young Hans was never particularly fond of the traditional approach to learning music. He didn't like being restricted by sheet music or formal training. In fact, Zimmer once said, "I was thrown out of eight schools, but I joined the choir because I liked it. I always thought that music was something you should create, not study."

Growing up in post-war Germany, Zimmer was also influenced by the rapidly changing world around him. The political and cultural shifts of the 1960s and 1970s, combined with the rise of television and film as popular forms of entertainment, began to shape his view of the world. Though music remained at the forefront of his interests, he didn't yet know that it would be his calling in life.

Discovering Music

Despite his early rebellion against structured piano lessons, Zimmer's love for music continued to grow. As a teenager, he discovered the wonders of electronic music and became fascinated with synthesizers. In the 1970s, electronic music was still relatively new, and Zimmer was drawn to the innovative sounds that could be created with technology. He would spend hours tinkering with instruments, experimenting with sounds, and learning how to combine them in new ways.

Hans zimmer

Zimmer's discovery of electronic music opened up a whole new world for him. He saw music not just as something that had to follow traditional rules, but as something that could be shaped and molded according to his imagination. This was a pivotal moment in his life, as it sparked his desire to create music in a way that was different from what he had been taught.

He also found inspiration in the progressive rock music of the time. Bands like Pink Floyd, Kraftwerk, and Tangerine Dream were pushing the boundaries of what music could be, using synthesizers and electronic instruments to create soundscapes that were unlike anything people had heard before. Zimmer's exposure to these influences would later play a significant role in shaping his own unique style.

Hans zimmer

From Keyboards to Composing

In his late teens, Zimmer began to see music as more than just a hobby. He started playing in bands and working as a session musician, performing on keyboards for various artists. His ability to use synthesizers made him stand out in the music scene, as few musicians at the time had mastered this new technology.

In the late 1970s, Zimmer moved to London, where he continued to develop his skills as a musician and composer. He joined the band The Buggles, which rose to fame with their hit song "Video Killed the Radio Star" in 1979. This song, which was the first-ever music video played on MTV, was a major success and gave

Hans zimmer

Zimmer his first taste of the music industry's global reach.

However, Zimmer quickly realized that while performing in bands was enjoyable, his true passion lay in creating music. He wanted to compose music that could tell a story, music that could evoke emotions in the listener. It was during this time that he began to explore the possibility of composing music for film and television.

Zimmer's background in electronic music, combined with his growing interest in storytelling through sound, made him well-suited for the world of film scoring. He had a unique ability to combine traditional instruments with electronic sounds, creating a musical style that was unlike anything else in the industry at the time. This fusion of classical and modern elements would later become a hallmark of his work, but in the early stages of his career, it was still something he was experimenting with.

As he continued to work in the music industry, Zimmer began to build a network of contacts in the world of film. He started composing music for commercials, television shows, and small films, gradually gaining experience and honing his craft. Each project allowed him to further develop his skills as a composer and learn how to use music to enhance visual storytelling.

By the early 1980s, Zimmer had fully transitioned from being a musician in a band to becoming a composer for film. His early work wasn't widely known at the time, but it provided him with the foundation he needed to take his career to the next level. Little did he know that his big break was just around the corner, and soon the world would recognize his immense talent.

This period of Zimmer's life set the stage for what would become one of the most successful and influential careers in film music history. His journey from a rebellious child who refused to follow traditional music lessons to a composer who would change the sound of cinema forever was only just beginning.

CHAPTER 2: BREAKING INTO THE INDUSTRY – MOVING TO LONDON

Hans Zimmer's move to London in the late 1970s marked a critical turning point in his life and career. London was a hub for creativity, with a vibrant music scene that was exploding with new sounds, genres, and artistic ideas. This was where punk, electronic, and rock music were all being redefined, and Zimmer found himself in the midst of this cultural explosion.

Arriving in London as a young musician with big dreams, Zimmer initially worked as a session musician. This allowed him to experiment with his love for synthesizers and electronic instruments, which were still relatively new and experimental at the time. London provided him with a platform to explore his musical identity, and it wasn't long before his unique style began to attract attention.

Zimmer's interest in technology and his fascination with blending electronic sounds with traditional music set him apart. While most composers were sticking to classical instruments, Zimmer embraced modern technology, using synthesizers to create sounds that felt fresh and innovative. London offered him opportunities to work with a variety of artists, and he became known for his ability to blend these different musical worlds together.

During his time in London, Zimmer worked with The Buggles, the band behind the iconic hit "Video Killed the Radio Star." This song became a global sensation and was famously the first music video ever played on MTV. Although Zimmer's role in the band was primarily as a keyboardist, this experience gave him valuable exposure to the international music industry and showed him the power of music on a global scale.

While playing in bands was an exciting part of his early career, Zimmer soon realized that his true passion was not in performing but in creating music. He wanted to compose, to write pieces that could tell a story and evoke emotion. London, with its diverse range of opportunities, allowed him to begin transitioning from being a musician to becoming a composer for film and television.

Early Collaborations and Influences

One of Zimmer's first major steps into the world of film music came when he started collaborating with Stanley Myers, an established composer known for his work on films like The Deer Hunter. Myers became a mentor to Zimmer, teaching him the intricacies of composing for film. Under Myers' guidance, Zimmer learned how to combine his electronic music background with more traditional orchestral elements, creating a unique sound that would become his signature.

Together, Zimmer and Myers worked on a number of films during the early 1980s, including Moonlighting and My Beautiful Laundrette. These films, while not blockbusters, gave Zimmer the experience he needed to understand the art of scoring a film. He learned how music could support and enhance the narrative of a story, becoming a critical part of the emotional experience for the audience.

Working with Myers also allowed Zimmer to develop his own voice as a composer. He began to explore how synthesizers could be used in film music, not just as a modern gimmick, but as a tool to evoke real emotion. This fusion of electronic and classical music set him apart from other composers of the time and caught the attention of filmmakers looking for something new.

Zimmer also found inspiration in other film composers, including Ennio Morricone and John Williams. Morricone's ability to use unconventional instruments and Williams' grand orchestral scores left a lasting impression on Zimmer. He admired how these composers used music to elevate the story, not just as background noise but as a central part of the narrative. Zimmer sought to do the same in his own work.

By the mid-1980s, Zimmer had built a solid reputation as a composer with a distinctive style. He was known for his ability to blend synthesizers with orchestras, creating a sound that was modern yet deeply emotional. His unique approach to film scoring would soon lead him to his first major breakthrough.

The Breakthrough with Rain Man

Hans zimmer

In 1988, Hans Zimmer's career took a giant leap forward when he was asked to compose the score for Rain Man, a film directed by Barry Levinson and starring Tom Cruise and Dustin Hoffman. This project was a game-changer for Zimmer, not only because the film went on to win the Academy Award for Best Picture, but also because his score became an iconic part of the movie's success.

The opportunity to score Rain Man came about in an unexpected way. Levinson had originally intended to use traditional classical music for the film, but when he heard Zimmer's experimental use of synthesizers, he was intrigued. Zimmer's approach was unconventional—he combined synthesized sounds with traditional instruments, creating a score that felt modern, minimalistic, and deeply emotional. Levinson took a chance on Zimmer, and it paid off in a big way.

Zimmer's score for Rain Man perfectly captured the mood of the film. The story of a man reconnecting with his autistic brother required music that was both sensitive and uplifting, and Zimmer delivered just that. His use of soft, melodic themes alongside electronic textures gave the film a unique sound that set it apart from other movies of the time. The music didn't overpower the story, but instead, it subtly enhanced the emotions on screen.

The success of Rain Man brought Zimmer widespread recognition. He was nominated for an Academy Award for Best Original Score, and suddenly, Hollywood's doors were wide open to him. Directors and producers began to take notice of Zimmer's work, and his phone started ringing with offers to score more films.

Zimmer's work on Rain Man also solidified his reputation as a composer who could bring something new and fresh to film music. His ability to blend electronic and acoustic elements became his signature style, and he quickly became one of the most sought-after composers in the industry.

This breakthrough marked the beginning of a new chapter in Zimmer's career. With Rain Man, Zimmer had shown the world that he was capable of creating music that was both innovative and deeply emotional. He had successfully carved out a space for himself in the competitive world of film scoring, and his journey as one of Hollywood's top composers

Hans zimmer

had just begun. The next few years would see Zimmer's influence grow as he collaborated with some of the most visionary filmmakers of his time, creating iconic scores that would define an era of cinema.

CHAPTER 3: CRAFTING A UNIQUE SOUND – SYNTHESIZERS AND THE ZIMMER STYLE

Hans Zimmer is often credited with revolutionizing film music, and one of the key elements of his groundbreaking style is his use of synthesizers. When Zimmer began working in the film industry, many composers were relying primarily on traditional orchestral instruments. Zimmer, however, saw the potential in synthesizers, which allowed him to create a broader range of sounds and moods. His innovative approach blended electronic music with classical elements, setting him apart from his peers.

Hans zimmer

Zimmer's love for synthesizers can be traced back to his teenage years when he first encountered electronic music. He saw synthesizers as tools that could be used not only to replicate traditional sounds but also to create entirely new sonic landscapes. This flexibility appealed to Zimmer, who was always looking for ways to push the boundaries of what film music could be.

In many of Zimmer's early scores, such as Rain Man and Driving Miss Daisy, the use of synthesizers helped him create a distinctive sound that combined warmth and modernity. This was especially important in films where he needed to evoke complex emotions. For Zimmer, synthesizers allowed him to tap into a range of feelings and atmospheres that were difficult to achieve with a traditional orchestra alone.

Hans zimmer

Combining Classical and Modern Sounds

While Zimmer is known for his love of technology, he has never completely abandoned traditional music. In fact, one of the reasons for his success is his ability to seamlessly combine classical instruments with electronic elements. This fusion has become a hallmark of Zimmer's work, creating scores that feel both timeless and modern.

Zimmer's use of orchestras is evident in some of his most iconic scores, such as Gladiator and The Dark Knight. In these films, he blends sweeping orchestral arrangements with

Hans zimmer

synthesizers and percussion to create music that is both grand and intimate. Zimmer's ability to mix these two musical worlds allows him to tell stories in a way that feels universal, transcending genres and appealing to a wide range of audiences.

This blending of classical and modern elements reflects Zimmer's broader philosophy of music. He doesn't see electronic and orchestral music as opposing forces but as tools that can be used together to create something new. For Zimmer, the goal is always to find the best way to tell a story through sound, and he uses whatever tools are available to achieve that.

Hans zimmer

Reinventing Film Music

Zimmer's approach to film music has had a lasting impact on the industry. By embracing technology and blending different musical styles, he has redefined what a film score can be. His work has influenced a generation of composers, many of whom have adopted his techniques and incorporated them into their own scores.

One of Zimmer's key contributions to film music is his belief that a score should do more than just support a film's visuals. For Zimmer, the music is an essential part of the storytelling process. His scores are often just as important as the dialogue or the action on screen, helping to

Hans zimmer

shape the emotional tone of a film and guide the audience through the story.

Zimmer's innovative approach has earned him a reputation as one of the most forward-thinking composers in the industry. He has constantly pushed the boundaries of what film music can be, and his willingness to experiment has led to some of the most memorable scores in modern cinema.

CHAPTER 4: COLLABORATING WITH FILMMAKERS – WORKING WITH RIDLEY SCOTT: GLADIATOR

One of Zimmer's most significant collaborations has been with director Ridley Scott, a partnership that has resulted in some of the most iconic film scores of all time. Their first major project together was Gladiator (2000), a historical epic that required a grand, emotional score to match its sweeping visuals.

For Gladiator, Zimmer created a score that perfectly captured the film's blend of action and emotion. The music for the film is both powerful and delicate, with moments of intense drama balanced by softer, more introspective pieces.

Hans zimmer

Zimmer's use of the voice of Lisa Gerrard, whose haunting vocals feature prominently in the score, added a layer of depth to the music, giving it an otherworldly quality that elevated the film's emotional impact.

The success of Gladiator helped cement Zimmer's reputation as a master of epic film scores, and his collaboration with Scott continued with other projects, including Black Hawk Down and Hannibal. Zimmer and Scott share a mutual understanding of how music can enhance a film's narrative, and their partnership has produced some of the most memorable film music of the past two decades.

Hans zimmer

The Iconic Partnership with Christopher Nolan

Zimmer's most famous and enduring collaboration has been with director Christopher Nolan. Their partnership began with Batman Begins in 2005 and has continued through some of Nolan's biggest films, including Inception, Interstellar, and Dunkirk. Together, they have created some of the most recognizable and innovative scores in modern cinema.

For Zimmer, working with Nolan has been an opportunity to push his creativity to new heights. Nolan's films often deal with complex themes and non-linear storytelling, and Zimmer's scores have played a crucial role in helping to guide audiences through these intricate narratives. The

Hans zimmer

music for Inception, for example, uses layers of sound to reflect the film's theme of dreams within dreams, while the score for Interstellar captures the vastness of space and the emotional weight of the film's story.

Zimmer and Nolan share a deep respect for each other's craft, and their collaboration has resulted in some of the most memorable moments in recent film history. Zimmer's ability to create music that enhances Nolan's visually striking films has made their partnership one of the most successful in the industry.

Scoring The Lion King and Winning an Oscar

Hans zimmer

One of Zimmer's most beloved scores is for the 1994 animated classic The Lion King. This project was a departure from Zimmer's usual work, as it required him to create music for an animated film aimed at a younger audience. However, Zimmer embraced the challenge and delivered a score that was both uplifting and emotionally resonant.

The music for The Lion King is deeply influenced by African rhythms and melodies, reflecting the film's setting. Zimmer collaborated with musicians from South Africa to ensure that the score was authentic, and his use of traditional African instruments helped to create a unique sound that set the film apart from other animated movies.

Hans zimmer

Zimmer's work on The Lion King earned him an Academy Award for Best Original Score, one of the highest honors in the film industry. The success of the film and its music cemented Zimmer's status as one of Hollywood's top composers, and the score remains one of his most popular works to this day.

Chapter 5: Music as a Storytelling Tool – How Zimmer's Scores Shape Film Narrative

For Hans Zimmer, music is more than just an accompaniment to a film's visuals. It is an essential part of the storytelling process. Zimmer's scores are often used to convey emotions, build tension, and create atmosphere, helping to guide the audience through the narrative of a film.

One of Zimmer's key techniques is his use of leitmotifs, or recurring musical themes, to represent different characters or ideas within a film. These themes evolve over the course of the movie, reflecting the growth and development of the characters. For example, in The Dark Knight Trilogy, Zimmer created a distinct musical theme for each of the major characters, using their respective themes to highlight their journeys and struggles.

Zimmer also uses music to shape the pacing of a film. His scores are often designed to build gradually, creating a sense of anticipation and suspense. This is particularly evident in films like Inception and Interstellar, where the music plays a crucial role in maintaining the film's tension and guiding the audience through complex, layered narratives.

Hans zimmer

Creating Emotion Through Sound

One of Zimmer's greatest strengths as a composer is his ability to evoke deep emotions through his music. Whether it's the sense of wonder and awe in Interstellar or the heart-wrenching sorrow in Gladiator, Zimmer's scores have a way of connecting with audiences on an emotional level.

Zimmer's approach to creating emotion through music often involves experimenting with different sounds and textures. He is known for using unconventional instruments and techniques to create unique sonic landscapes that enhance the emotional impact of a film. For example, in Dunkirk, Zimmer used a ticking watch to create a sense of urgency and tension, while in The Lion King, he used African drums and vocals to evoke the spirit of the savannah.

By combining these elements with more traditional orchestral music, Zimmer is able to create scores that resonate with audiences long after the film has ended. His ability to tap into universal emotions through sound is one of the reasons why his music has had such a lasting impact on both the film industry and popular culture.

Building Suspense and Drama

Zimmer's use of music to build suspense is one of his trademarks. In many of his films, the music plays a crucial role in creating tension and drama, often driving the action forward and keeping audiences on the edge of their seats.

Zimmer's score for The Dark Knight is a perfect example of this. The music in the film is dark and brooding, with a constant sense of impending danger. Zimmer uses repetitive, minimalist themes to create a feeling of unease, building the tension until it reaches a climax. The use of dissonance and harsh, metallic sounds adds to the sense of chaos, perfectly matching the tone of the film.

Similarly, in Inception, Zimmer's score is designed to reflect the layers of the dream world. The music builds in intensity as the characters descend deeper into the dream, creating a sense of urgency and danger. The iconic "BRAM" sound, which became a hallmark of the film, is

Hans zimmer

used to heighten the drama and give the audience a visceral experience of the dream collapsing.

Zimmer's ability to build suspense and drama through his music has made him one of the most sought-after composers in the film industry. His scores not only enhance the visual storytelling but also create an immersive experience for the audience, drawing them deeper into the narrative. Whether it's the ticking tension of Dunkirk or the dreamlike layers of Inception, Zimmer knows how to use music to keep viewers engaged and emotionally invested.

CHAPTER 6: THE TECHNOLOGY OF SOUND – INNOVATIONS IN MUSIC PRODUCTION

Hans Zimmer is known not only for his creative compositions but also for his pioneering use of technology in music production. He has always embraced new tools and techniques, constantly seeking ways to expand the boundaries of what is possible in film scoring. One of his biggest contributions to modern film music is his use of digital instruments and advanced sound design technologies, which have allowed him to craft scores that sound unlike anything else.

Zimmer was one of the first major film composers to fully embrace digital workstations

Hans zimmer

and software for composing, editing, and producing music. He has worked with computer-based music technologies since the 1980s, long before they became the industry standard. His studio, Remote Control Productions, is a hub for cutting-edge music technology, where Zimmer and his team experiment with new methods of sound production.

Using digital instruments has allowed Zimmer to create sounds that would be impossible or difficult to achieve with traditional instruments. This innovation is one of the reasons his scores are so distinct. By blending digital and acoustic elements, Zimmer creates complex soundscapes that add layers of depth and texture to his music.

Hans zimmer

The Role of Digital Instruments

Digital instruments have played a significant role in shaping Zimmer's sound. From synthesizers to virtual orchestras, these tools have given Zimmer the ability to explore new musical ideas and experiment with different textures and atmospheres. Unlike traditional instruments, which have fixed tones and limits, digital instruments can be manipulated in countless ways, offering endless creative possibilities.

Zimmer has used digital instruments to evoke a variety of moods and settings in his films. For example, in Interstellar, he used digital organs to create a sense of awe and wonder, blending them with traditional orchestral music to give the score an otherworldly quality. In Inception, Zimmer employed synthesizers and digital brass sounds to convey the mind-bending nature of the film's dream sequences, creating a sense of scale and complexity that mirrored the story's structure.

Zimmer's ability to seamlessly integrate digital instruments with traditional ones has made his scores sound modern and timeless at the same time. His work has inspired a generation of composers to explore the creative potential of technology in their own music, pushing the boundaries of what film scores can achieve.

Experimenting with New Sounds

Hans zimmer

Hans Zimmer's curiosity and willingness to experiment are at the core of his success. Throughout his career, he has constantly sought new sounds and ways to enhance the emotional impact of his scores. Zimmer is known for using unconventional instruments and objects to create unique sonic textures that fit the specific tone of each film.

For example, in The Dark Knight, Zimmer experimented with razor blades on piano strings to create the unsettling, metallic sound associated with the character of the Joker. This eerie, distorted noise reflected the chaotic and dangerous nature of the villain, adding to the psychological intensity of the film. In Dunkirk, Zimmer used a ticking watch to build tension, symbolizing the constant passage of time as soldiers desperately awaited rescue.

Hans zimmer

Zimmer's willingness to step outside the bounds of traditional music composition and incorporate unexpected sounds has led to some of the most memorable and distinctive film scores in recent history. His relentless experimentation ensures that each score feels fresh and tailored to the specific needs of the film.

CHAPTER 7: ZIMMER'S MOST ICONIC SCORES – INCEPTION: DREAM LAYERS IN MUSIC

One of Hans Zimmer's most iconic and complex scores is Christopher Nolan's Inception (2010). The film's narrative revolves around dreams within dreams, and Zimmer's music mirrors this intricate structure. The score is built on layers, much like the film's plot, and creates a sense of depth and complexity that enhances the storytelling.

The famous "BRAM" sound, which became synonymous with Inception, is a low, thunderous noise that punctuates key moments in the film. This sound was achieved by manipulating a slowed-down version of Édith Piaf's song "Non, Je Ne Regrette Rien," which plays an important role in the film's narrative. The use of time-stretched music in this way reflects the theme of time dilation in the dream world.

Zimmer's score for Inception also features recurring motifs that are used to signify different levels of the dream. As the characters descend deeper into the dream layers, the music builds in intensity, creating a sense of urgency and tension. The use of electronic sounds, combined with traditional orchestral elements, gives the score a futuristic feel, perfectly complementing the film's high-concept narrative.

Hans zimmer

The Epic Journey of Interstellar

Interstellar (2014), another collaboration with Christopher Nolan, presented Zimmer with the challenge of scoring a film that explores humanity's place in the cosmos. The film is vast in scope, dealing with themes of love, time, and survival, and Zimmer's score plays a critical role in conveying the emotional and philosophical depth of the story.

Zimmer used an organ as the central instrument in the Interstellar score, an unconventional choice that adds a sense of grandeur and spirituality to the music. The organ, traditionally associated with churches and solemn occasions, helps to evoke the awe-inspiring scale of space and the characters' search for meaning in the universe. The use of minimalism and repetitive motifs gives the score a meditative quality, while also building tension in the film's most dramatic moments.

One of the most striking elements of the Interstellar score is its use of silence and quiet. Zimmer intentionally left space in the music to reflect the vastness of space and the loneliness of the character's journey. This restraint makes the louder, more intense moments even more powerful, creating a dynamic score that is both emotional and thought-provoking.

The Heroic Themes of The Dark Knight Trilogy

Hans zimmer

Hans Zimmer's collaboration with Christopher Nolan on The Dark Knight Trilogy (2005–2012) produced some of the most iconic superhero music of all time. Unlike traditional superhero scores, which are often triumphant and grand, Zimmer's music for Batman Begins, The Dark Knight, and The Dark Knight Rises is dark, intense, and psychological, reflecting the complex nature of the film's protagonist, Bruce Wayne.

Zimmer's approach to the score for The Dark Knight Trilogy was to focus on the internal struggles of the characters rather than the external action. The music for Batman is brooding and minimalist, with a sense of restraint that mirrors the character's inner turmoil. For the Joker, Zimmer created an entirely different sound—chaotic, unpredictable, and dissonant, using razor-sharp strings to evoke the character's insanity.

The score for The Dark Knight is particularly notable for its use of two notes to represent Batman. This simple, minimalist motif is repeated throughout the trilogy, evolving with the character as he grows and changes. The music becomes more heroic in The Dark Knight Rises, reflecting Batman's journey from vigilante to symbol of hope.

From Fantasy to Reality: Dune

Zimmer's score for Denis Villeneuve's Dune (2021) marks another significant achievement in his career. Dune is a science fiction epic based

Hans zimmer

on Frank Herbert's novel, and Zimmer's music was instrumental in bringing the vast, otherworldly universe of the story to life.

For Dune, Zimmer drew inspiration from Middle Eastern and North African music, using a wide range of instruments, including vocals, wind instruments, and percussion, to create a soundscape that felt both ancient and futuristic. The score is textured and atmospheric, with layers of sound that reflect the desert planet of Arrakis and the mystical nature of the story. Zimmer's use of vocal chants and unconventional instruments gives the score a primal, elemental quality that mirrors the themes of power, destiny, and survival in Dune. The music plays a crucial role in immersing the audience in the film's world, making it feel real and lived-in, despite its fantastical setting.

CHAPTER 8: A GLOBAL INFLUENCE – ZIMMER'S IMPACT ON FILM MUSIC WORLDWIDE

Hans Zimmer's influence extends far beyond Hollywood. His innovative approach to film scoring has had a global impact, inspiring composers around the world to experiment with new sounds and techniques. Zimmer's blend of classical, electronic, and world music elements has redefined what film music can be, and his scores have set a new standard for cinematic storytelling through sound.

Zimmer's work has been particularly influential in countries with growing film industries, such as India, South Korea, and China. Many composers in these regions have adopted Zimmer's approach of blending traditional instruments with modern technology, creating scores that reflect their own cultural identities while also appealing to international audiences.

Zimmer's global influence is also evident in the number of international filmmakers who seek him out for their projects. From French directors like Denis Villeneuve to Chinese filmmakers, Zimmer's reputation as a visionary composer has made him a sought-after collaborator in the global film industry.

Hans zimmer

Mentoring the Next Generation of Composers

One of Zimmer's most significant contributions to the film-music industry is his role as a mentor to up-and-coming composers. Through his studio, Remote Control Productions, Zimmer has helped to nurture the talents of many young composers who have gone on to become successful in their own right.

Zimmer's approach to mentorship is hands-on, often inviting young composers to work alongside him on major film projects. He encourages them to experiment with new sounds and techniques, pushing them to think outside the box and develop their own unique voices. Many of Zimmer's protégés, including composers like Lorne Balfe, Ramin Djawadi, and Benjamin Wallfisch, have gone on to score major films and television series on their own, contributing to the next generation of innovative film music. These composers, while influenced by Zimmer's work, have developed distinct styles that carry forward his legacy of experimentation and blending of musical genres. Zimmer's willingness to share his knowledge and experience has created a network of composers who continue to push the boundaries of film scoring.

CHAPTER 9: THE LEGACY OF HANS ZIMMER – REDEFINING THE SOUND OF MODERN CINEMA

Hans Zimmer's impact on the world of film music is immeasurable. Over the course of his career, he has redefined what film scores can be, moving away from the traditional orchestral sound to create something entirely new. By blending digital and acoustic elements, incorporating unconventional instruments, and constantly experimenting with sound design, Zimmer has set a new standard for what film music can achieve.

One of Zimmer's most lasting contributions is his ability to use music to tell stories. His scores are not just background noise; they are integral to the narrative, adding emotional depth, building tension, and enhancing the viewer's connection to the characters and the world of the film. Zimmer's music has the power to move audiences in ways that go beyond words, creating an emotional resonance that stays with them long after the credits roll.

Awards and Accolades

Zimmer's innovative approach to film scoring has earned him numerous accolades throughout his career. He has won an Academy Award, several Golden Globes, Grammys, and BAFTAs, among other prestigious honors. Despite these awards, Zimmer has remained humble, often crediting the collaborative nature of filmmaking for his success. He views each score as a team effort, where his music plays a crucial part in the overall storytelling process.

In 2022, Zimmer won his second Academy Award for his score for Dune, nearly three decades after his first Oscar win for The Lion King. This achievement highlights his enduring influence in the industry and his ability to remain relevant across different genres and generations.

Zimmer's Music in Popular Culture

Beyond the world of cinema, Zimmer's music has become a part of popular culture. His scores

Hans zimmer

for films like The Lion King, Pirates of the Caribbean, and The Dark Knight have transcended the screen, becoming recognizable and beloved pieces of music in their own right. Zimmer's music has been used in trailers, commercials, and even sports events, further cementing its place in the broader cultural landscape.

Zimmer's music is also frequently performed in concerts, both as part of film music festivals and in standalone performances. His live concerts, where he performs with an orchestra and a band, have become popular events, allowing fans to experience his music in a new and exciting way. These concerts often feature multimedia elements, including film clips, lights, and visual effects, creating a cinematic experience for the audience.

Hans zimmer

The Zimmer Legacy

As Hans Zimmer continues to compose and innovate, his legacy as one of the most important and influential film composers of all time is already secure. His work has transformed the way we think about film music, making it an integral part of the storytelling process rather than just an accompaniment to the visuals. Zimmer's scores are iconic, memorable, and emotionally powerful, leaving a lasting impression on audiences and filmmakers alike. Zimmer's legacy is not only in his own music but also in the countless composers he has inspired and mentored. Through his work, he has changed the way music is created and experienced in film, ensuring that his influence will be felt for generations to come.

CHAPTER 10: THE MAN BEHIND THE MUSIC – A LIFE DEDICATED TO CREATIVITY

Behind the scores and the fame, Hans Zimmer is a man deeply dedicated to his craft. His passion for music and storytelling drives everything he does, from composing to mentoring. Zimmer's career has been defined by a constant desire to learn, innovate, and push the boundaries of what is possible in music. He is not content with resting on his laurels; instead, he approaches each new project as an opportunity to explore new ideas and sounds.

Zimmer's work ethic is legendary, often spending long hours in the studio to perfect his scores. Despite his success, he remains down-to-earth and approachable, always willing to collaborate and share his knowledge with others. Zimmer's humility and generosity have earned him the respect of his peers and the admiration of fans around the world.

Personal Life and Values

While Zimmer's professional achievements are well-known, he has kept his personal life relatively private. What is known is that he is a dedicated father and family man, and he values the time he spends with his children. Zimmer often speaks about the importance of balance in his life, ensuring that he makes time for his family despite the demands of his career.

Zimmer is also deeply passionate about environmental issues, often using his platform to raise awareness about the need to protect the planet. He has supported various environmental causes over the years, reflecting his belief that music and art can inspire people to care about the world around them.

The Future of Hans Zimmer

As Hans Zimmer continues to work on new projects, it's clear that his passion for music and storytelling remains as strong as ever. He has several upcoming film scores in the works, and there's no doubt that he will continue to push the boundaries of what film music can achieve.

Zimmer's legacy as a composer, innovator, and mentor is secure, but his story is far from over. As long as there are stories to tell, Hans Zimmer will be there to provide the music that brings them to life. Whether in the world of cinema or beyond, Zimmer's influence will continue to resonate, inspiring future generations of composers and music lovers alike.

CONCLUSION

Hans Zimmer's journey from a young boy in Germany, playing keyboards and discovering the magic of music, to becoming one of the most influential film composers of all time is nothing short of extraordinary. His career has redefined what it means to compose for the screen, blending classical traditions with modern technologies to create music that is both innovative and emotionally powerful. Zimmer's work has become an integral part of storytelling, transforming how we experience films and how music shapes our emotional connection to the characters, worlds, and narratives we see on screen.

Hans zimmer

Through decades of hard work, experimentation, and collaboration, Zimmer has composed some of the most iconic film scores in history, from the awe-inspiring themes of Gladiator and The Lion King to the haunting melodies of Interstellar and the mind-bending soundscapes of Inception. His scores go beyond merely supporting the visual experience; they elevate the storytelling, helping to define the atmosphere, emotions, and rhythms of the films he works on.

What makes Hans Zimmer's work so remarkable is his ability to adapt, grow, and innovate continuously. He has embraced new technologies, from synthesizers to digital production tools, always exploring new ways to create sound that resonates deeply with audiences. His music has become a bridge between the classical and the modern, the traditional and the experimental, creating a sound that is uniquely his own. He has demonstrated that film music can stand on its own as a form of art, capable of moving people in ways that transcend language and culture.

Zimmer's influence extends beyond the scores he has written. Through his collaborations with filmmakers and his mentorship of young composers, he has shaped the next generation of film music. His influence can be seen in the works of numerous composers who are inspired by his ability to combine emotion, narrative, and technical innovation in ways that redefine how we hear and feel movies.

As the live performances of his music continue to draw fans from around the world, Zimmer's legacy grows even more profound. His concerts bring the magic of film music to the stage, allowing audiences to experience the full impact of his compositions in a new and immersive way. These performances celebrate not just Zimmer's music but the role that music plays in our lives as a powerful force for storytelling, emotion, and connection.

The legacy of Hans Zimmer will be felt for generations to come, both in the world of cinema and beyond. His scores have changed the way we understand and appreciate film music, showing us that a great score is more than just an accompaniment—it is a vital part of the storytelling process. As long as there are stories to tell and films to score, the influence of Hans Zimmer will continue to inspire, captivate, and move audiences around the world.

Hans zimmer

In the end, Hans Zimmer's life and work remind us that music has the power to tell stories, evoke emotions, and bring people together in ways that few other art forms can. His genius lies not just in his ability to compose extraordinary music, but in his understanding that music, at its core, is a storytelling force that connects us all.

www.ingramcontent.com/pod-product-compliance
Lightning Source LLC
LaVergne TN
LVHW021449231224
799792LV00005B/471